THE METHOD OF PRESERVING THE FACE OF RIGPA, THE ESSENCE OF WISDOM

AN ASPECT OF TRAINING IN THOROUGH CUT
BY JU MIPHAM NAMGYAL

TONY DUFF

PADMA KARPO TRANSLATION COMMITTEE

This text is secret and should not be shown to those who have not had the necessary introduction and instructions of the Thorough Cut system of Dzogchen meditation. If you have not had the necessary instructions, reading this text can be harmful to your spiritual health! Seal. Seal. Seal.

First edition, Januart 2009
ISBN: 978-9937-8244-1-5

Janson typeface with diacritical marks and
Tibetan Classic typeface
Designed and created by Tony Duff
Tibetan Computer Company
http://www.tibet.dk/tcc

Produced, Printed, and Published by
Padma Karpo Translation Committee
P.O. Box 4957
Kathmandu
NEPAL

Web-site and e-mail contact through:
http://www.tibet.dk/pktc
or search Padma Karpo Translation Committee on the web.

CONTENTS

INTRODUCTION v

THE METHOD OF PRESERVING THE FACE OF RIGPA,
THE ESSENCE OF WISDOM BY JU MIPHAM
NAMGYAL 1

GLOSSARY 5

TIBETAN TEXT 13

INTRODUCTION

This is a text by the great Nyingma scholar-practitioner Ju Mipham Namgyal [1846–1912]. Mipham, as he is usually called, has become the most well-known of Nyingma scholars. He is so well known these days that no further introduction to him should be needed. The text itself is drawn from *The Collected Works* of Mipham.

Generally speaking, his text here concerns the practice of the innermost level of Great Completion[1]. The innermost level of Great Completion has two main practices, one called Thorough Cut and one called Direct Crossing. Of the two, this text concerns itself with the practice of Thorough Cut.

More specifically, the content of the text can be understood through its title, *The Method of Preserving the Face of Rigpa, The Essence of Wisdom*. The title has two parts, the main title and the poetic sub-title. The main title, "The Method of Preserving the Face of Rigpa" tells us that this text focusses

---

[1] Tib. rdzogs chen. Dzogchen.

on one specific aspect of Thorough Cut practice; it focusses
on the essential technique within the practice called "preserving rigpa". The poetic sub-title, "The Essence of Wisdom"
refers to the fact that the technique of preserving rigpa really
is the most essential technique of all techniques needed for
developing wisdom.

"Preserving" is an important term in both Essence Mahamudra and Great Completion[2] teaching. It refers to maintaining
and not losing a particular state either of mind or essence of
mind. There is a little more about it in the glossary though
reading the text should help you to get a further feeling for
the word. Note that this term is not only used in the context
of maintaining the profound essence of mind; it is a more
general term than that. It has the sense of "there is a state of
mind that the instructions are telling you has to be brought
forth—high, low, or otherwise—and, once it has been brought forth, you have to preserve and maintain that, nurturing
it to the extent that you are capable". The idea of nurturing
is important.

The text was written for those practising the Thorough Cut
of Great Completion and these days it is a popular in the
Nyingma tradition for teaching and learning the subject.
More often than not it is read as a support for the teaching
contained in another of Mipham's texts on this subject, the
very well-known *The Way of the Realized Old Dogs, Advice that
Points out the Essence of Mind, called "A Lamp that Dispels the
Darkness*. We have translated that text too and published it as

---

[2] Tib. rdzogs pa chen po.

a book so that Western practitioners can have access to these texts which are a core part of the transmission these days of the Thorough Cut teaching[3].

Even though this text was written as an explanation of Thorough Cut practice, the instruction is equally applicable to Essence Mahamudra. In fact, this exact same instruction is mentioned by Gampopa when teaching his senior disciples, Dusum Khyenpa, and so on[4]. For this most essential part of the practice, the words and examples used are exactly the same in both the Thorough Cut Great Completion and Essence Mahamudra systems of teaching.

Overview of the Text

There is a short set of instructions which sum up the whole path of Thorough Cut (and Essence Mahamudra, too). It is: "Recognize, Train, and Finalize"[5]. The first instruction means that you have, initially, to be introduced to[6], and

---

[3] Authored by Tony Duff, published by Padma Karpo Translation Committee, first edition, 2009.

[4] See the book by Tony Duff, published by Padma Karpo Translation Committee, of the questions and answers between Gampopa and four of his main, yogin disciples.

[5] This instruction is explained much more extensively in the book *Ground, Path, and Fruition* containing teachings of Tsoknyi Rinpoche. It is authored by Tony Duff, published by Padma Karpo Translation Committee in 2006.

[6] Introduction to the nature of mind is mostly mis-translated
(continued...)

because of that, recognize rigpa[7]. The second means that, after that, you have to train it up, bringing it fully to life within you[8]. The third says that, if you continue with that training, it will bring you to the completion of the path, the fruition level[9]. Those three points are the skeleton around which the instruction is given in the text and in fact, Mipham's text is as much an explanation of these three instructions as it is an explanation of preserving rigpa. If you look for these three topics as you read the text, you will be get a much better understanding of the meaning of the text than if you were to look specifically for the topic of preservation.

The first step of introduction and recognition is a whole topic in itself and he does not say much about here. Our book *Peak Doorways to Emancipation*[10] contains a whole text which looks into this topic in depth. Patrul Rinpoche's *Feature of the Glorious, Expert King*[11] and his commentary to it also makes this step of the practice very clear.

---

[6](...continued)
these days as "pointing out" instruction.

[7] Tib. ngo shes pa.

[8] Tib. rtsal sbyong ba.

[9] Tib. brtan pa thob pa.

[10] Authored by Tony Duff, published by Padma Karpo Translation Committee in 2008.

[11] Authored by Tony Duff, published by Padma Karpo Translation Committee in a second, revised edition, in 2008.

Ju Mipham Namgyal
Mural on the wall of Dzogchen Monastery, Tibet,
2007. Photograph by the author.

The emphasis in this text is on the second step, the training step. The rigpa which has been recognized now has to be brought fully to life. To train it up, the practitioner engages in the process of preserving the face of the rigpa which has at least been recognized, even if it is not very operational. Hence the name of the text "The Method of Preserving the Face of Rigpa". The way to preserve it is described through a standard, three-part progression of increasing ability to liberate the discursive thoughts which are the face of not rigpa[12].

The final step, means that the training has a completion. At that point when the training has been finalized, one has only the wisdom of a buddha. Essentially speaking, the wisdom was arrived at through the most essential practice of preserving the rigpa, hence the second part of the title "The Essence of Wisdom".

Our Supports for Study

I have been encouraged over the years by all of my teachers and gurus to pass on some of the knowledge I have accumulated in a lifetime dedicated to the study and practice, primarily through the Tibetan Buddhist tradition, of Buddhism. On the one hand they have encouraged me to teach. On the other hand, they are concerned that, while many general books on Buddhism have been and are being published, there are few books that present the actual texts of the tradition.

---

[12] The usual translation of not rigpa is "ignorance" but in fact, it literally means "not being in rigpa".

They and many other, closely involved people have encouraged me to make and publish high quality translations of individual texts of the tradition.

In general, we have published a wide range of books that present the important literature of Tibetan Buddhism. In particular, the author of this text was one of the important figures in the transmission of the most profound Great Completion teachings in Tibet and we have published many of the important texts of that system, with each one carefully selected to inform about a particular aspect of that teaching. This text lays out the system of Thorough Cut practice briefly. Another of our publications with a text by Mipham but which has a more extensive treatment of the material is the very famous *Way of the Realized Old Dogs*; we strongly recommend reading it in conjunction with this text. Other publication from us that lay out the whole system and which are important to read in conjunction with this one are *The Feature of the Glorious, Expert King* by Patrul Rinpoche, *About the Three Lines* by Dodrupchen III, *Alchemy of Accomplishment* by Dudjom Jigdral Yeshe Dorje, *Hinting at Dzogchen* by Tony Duff, *Peak Doorways to Emancipation* by Shakya Shri, and so on.

All in all, you will find many books both for free and for sale on our web-site, all of them prepared to the highest level of quality. Many of our books are available not only on paper but as electronic editions that can be downloaded, and all of them are prepared to the highest level of quality. We encourage you to look at our web-site to see what we have; the address is on the copyright page at the front of this book. Major book sellers also carry our paper editions.

It has also been a project of ours to make tools that non-Tibetans and Tibetans alike could use for the study and translation of Tibetan texts. As part of that project, we prepare electronic editions of Tibetan texts in the Tibetan Text input office of the Padma Karpo Translation Committee and make them available to the world. Tibetan texts are often corrupt so we make a special point of carefully correcting our work before making it available through our web-site. Thus, our electronic texts are not careless productions like most Tibetan texts found on the web but are highly reliable editions that can be used by non-scholars and scholars alike. Moreover, many of the texts are free. The Tibetan text for this book is available for download as a free, electronic edition. It is also included at the back of the book as an aid to serious study.

Our electronic texts can be read, searched, and so on, using our Tibetan software. The software can be used to set up a reference library of these texts and then used to read and even research them quickly and easily. The software, called TibetD and TibetDoc, has many special features that make it useful not only for reading but also for understanding and even translating texts. One key feature is that you can highlight a Tibetan term in a text then look it up immediately in any of our electronic dictionaries. We suggest the highly acclaimed *Illuminator Tibetan-English Dictionary* as the best dictionary for the purpose. As with all of our publications, the software and electronic texts can be obtained from our web-site whose address is on the copyright page at the front of the book.

Health Warning

The text here is about a subject that is kept secret. Therefore, I have translated the text as it is, providing enough notes so that someone who does understand the meaning could understand the translation without mistake. However, I have deliberately not given any further explanation of or commentary to the meaning. Anyone who has had these teachings in person will be able to understand them or at least go to their teacher and ask for further explanation. Anyone who has heard these teachings in person from a qualified teacher, and especially who has had the introduction to the nature of mind around which the teachings hinge, please use and enjoy the texts as you will. However, if you have not heard these teachings and if you have not had a proper introduction to the nature of your mind, you would be better off not reading this book but seeking out someone who could teach it to you. These days there are both non-Tibetans and Tibetans who can do that for you and who are available in many countries across our planet. In short, the contents of this book could be dangerous to your spiritual health if you are not ready for it, so exercise care.

These days, in the times of rampant globalization, these deep secrets have become very public. That is not necessarily a good thing. For example, I have many times in the last few years run into young men who are extremely confident of their understanding of the meaning of these profound systems but who just spout words that they have read in books. Unfortunately, they have read the books and know the words but have not contacted the inner meaning that the books are intended to be merely a pointer towards. The solidity of their minds is noticeable and not being helped by reading these things that they are not ready for and should not be reading.

My best wishes to all of you.
May you preserve the state!

Lama Tony Duff
Padma Karpo Translation Committee
Swayambunath,
Nepal
January, 2009

THE METHOD OF PRESERVING THE FACE OF RIGPA, THE ESSENCE OF WISDOM

by Ju Mipham Namgyal

Homage to the glorious, Primordial Protector[13].

The training of rigpa comes in three steps: recognition, training, and finalization.

First, using the guru's oral instruction you home in on the naked face of rigpa until it is seen clearly without mental analysis[14]. When that has been settled, you yourself training in that essence is the only thing of importance. In other

---

[13] The primordial protector is ones own mind at its very origin. It protects you fundamentally speaking. If put into the form of a deity, it will be Samantabhadra in this system or Great Vajradhara in the Mahamudra system.

[14] This means "... home in on the naked face of rigpa until you see it clearly without any of the coverings of dualistic mind's conceptual style of mental analysis which, if present, would distort the view of rigpa".

words, just to recognize it is not sufficient, it must be trained up fully.

Proceeding with that, you have initially recognized rigpa but, when you begin resting in it, the hindrances of discursive thought make it difficult for naked rigpa to shine forth[15]. So at that time, it is important to lengthen the period of staying in the state of uncontrived rigpa by resting in it again and again and without any stopping or furthering of discursive thoughts while doing it[16]. By habituating yourself to it like that again and again the waves of discursive thought will subside in strength and rigpa itself will grow clearer. When that has happened, stay equipoised on it as much as you can and, in post-equipoise, rely on mindfulness which recalls rigpa itself[17].

By habituating yourself to that, rigpa will be trained up further and further. Initially, discursive thoughts will arise. However, there is no need to rely on an antidote other than themselves to stop them; just by leaving them in their own place, they will be self-liberated in a few moments, like a

---

[15] Shine forth is a term that does not just mean appear but means specifically to appear within mind.

[16] While doing this, you do not engage in the usual approach of cultivating something newly, in which you use thoughts to stop that which is seen to be opposite to what you want to achieve and to further what you want to achieve. If you did, it would all be contrivance and, as he says, this is about non-contrivance.

[17] Recalls here does not mean think about, it means "returns you to".

coiled-up snake that by itself uncoils itself. After further habituation, discursive thoughts will arise as small disturbances but will also immediately fade of themselves, like a drawing on water. Even further habituation to that state will result in the discursive thoughts arising without doing any harm at all. The resulting lack of hope or fear over whether discursive thoughts arise or not will come forth as an experience in which they have no effect, being neither helpful nor harmful, like a thief who enters an empty house[18].

By even further habituation to that state, the process of training comes to its conclusion: finally, discursive thoughts and the alaya[19] together with its movement-producing winds dissolve into the uncontrived dharmakaya and rigpa has been captured in its place. Like ordinary earth and rocks cannot be found on an island of gold even if you search for them, every appearance and existence without exception now shines forth as the realm of dharmakaya, having become universal purity. This point is called, "finalization"[20]. At this point, the hopes

---

[18] The thief comes but does no harm because the house is empty. His coming on the other hand also does not improve the situation. In short, the arrival of thought has no effect, one way or another, on the experienced state.

[19] For more about the complicated subject of alaya, see Mipham's other text, mentioned in the introduction, *The Way of the Realized Old Dogs, Advice that Points out the Essence of Mind, called "A Lamp that Dispels the Darkness.*

[20] Tib. brtan pa thob. This is the third of the three part process of recognizing, training, and finalization.

and fears of samsara and nirvana, and of birth and death have been destroyed from the root.

As with that progression in which daytime appearances and discursive thoughts are gradually brought under the control of rigpa, so the night-time equivalents—the apprehension of dreams, fine and thick luminosity in them, and so on—will, without needing to rely on any other type of instruction come along[21]. Having understood that, you absolutely must, for as long as you have not finalized the practice, have unwavering perseverance in it, perseverance that is continuous, like the flow of a river.

Instruction given by Mipham. May virtue and goodness increase. Goodness!

Translated at Tsoknyi Rinpoche's request after receiving instruction on the text by Tony Duff of the Padma Karpo Translation Committee, July 6, 1996, at Swayambunath, Kathmandu, Nepal.

---

[21] The night-time equivalents are the experiences and realizations that come from night-time practices, such as being able to recognize dreams, then having degrees of luminosity mixed with dreams, and what follows on from that. There are many types of practice for utilizing dreams as part of the path. However, in this case, none of these types of instruction will be followed. The instruction already given covers both daytime and nighttime situations, equally.

GLOSSARY

Alaya, Tib. kun gzhi: This term, if translated, is usually translated as all-base or thereabouts. It is a Sanskrit term that means a range that underlies and forms a basis for something else. In Buddhist teaching, it means a particular level of mind that sits beneath all other levels of mind. However, it is used in several different ways in the Buddhist teaching and changes to a different meaning in case. In the Great Completion teachings, a distinction is made between alaya and alaya consciousness; the distinction is subtle but the two must not be confused.

Clinging, Tib. zhen pa: In Buddhism, this term refers specifically to the twofold process of dualistic mind mis-taking things that are not true, not pure, as true, pure, etcetera and then, because of seeing them as highly desirable even though they are not, attaching itself to or clinging to those things. This type of clinging acts as a kind of glue that keeps you with the unsatisfactory things of cyclic existence because of mistakenly seeing them as desirable.

Contrivance, contrived, Tib. bcos pa: A term meaning that something has been altered from its native state.

Cyclic existence, Skt. saṃsāra, Tib. 'khor ba: The type of existence
that sentient beings have which is that they continue on from
one existence to another, always within the enclosure of
births that are produced by ignorance and experienced as
unsatisfactory. Although the Tibetan term literally means
"cycling", the original Sanskrit has a slightly different meaning; it means to go about, here and there.

Dharmakaya, Tib. chos sku: The mind of a buddha. Dharma here
means reality, what actually is, and kāya means body.

Discursive thought, Skt. vikalpita, Tib. rnam rtog: This means
more than just the superficial thought that is heard as a voice
in the head. It includes the entirety of conceptual process
that arises due to mind contacting any object of any of the
senses. The Sanskrit and Tibetan literally mean "(dualistic)
thought (that arises from the mind wandering among the)
various (superficies perceived in the doors of the senses)".

Equipoise and post-attainment, Tib. mnyam bzhag and rjes thob:
Although often called "meditation and post-meditation", the
actual term is "equipoise and post-attainment". There is
great meaning in the actual wording which is lost by the
looser translation.

Essence, Tib. ngo bo: This is a key term used throughout Buddhist theory. The original in Sanskrit and the term in Tibetan, too, has both meanings of "essence" and "entity". In
some situations the term has more the first meaning and in
others, the second. For example, when speaking of mind and
mind's essence, it is referring to the core or essential part
within mind. On the other hand, when speaking of something such as fire, one can speak of the entity, fire, and its
characteristics, such as heat, and so on; in this case, the term
does not mean essence but means that thing, what is actually
is.

Foremost instruction, Skt. upadeśha, Tib. man ngag: there are several types of instruction mentioned in Buddhist literature: there is the general level of instruction which is the meaning contained in the words of the texts of the tradition; on a more personal and direct level there is oral instruction which has been passed down from teacher to student from the time of the buddha; and on the most profound level there is upadeśha which are not only oral instructions provided by one's guru but are special, core instructions that come out of personal experience and which convey the teaching concisely and with the full weight of personal experience. Upadeśha are crucial to the Vajra Vehicle because these are the special way of passing on the profound instructions needed for the student's realization.

Key points, Tib. gnad: Key points are those places in one's being that one works, like pressing buttons, in order to get some desired effect. For example, in meditation, there are key points of the body; by adjusting those key points, the mind is brought closer to reality and the meditation is thus assisted.

In general, this term is used in Buddhist meditation instruction but it is, in particular, part of the special vocabulary of the Great Completion teachings. Overall, the Great Completion teachings are given as a series of key points that must be attended to in order to bring forth the various realizations of the path.

Liveliness, Tib. rtsal: A key term in both Mahāmudrā and Great Completion. The term means the ability that something has to express itself. In the case of rigpa, it refers to how the rigpa actually comes out into expression. The term is sometimes translated as "display" but that is not right. It is not merely the display that is being talked about here but the fact that something has the ability to express itself in a certain way. Another English word that fits the meaning, though one which is drier than "liveliness" is "expressivity". In the end, given the way that this term is actually used in the higher tantras, it refers to the liveliness of whatever is being referred to, usually rigpa.

Luminosity, Skt. prabhāsvara, Tib. 'od gsal ba: the core of mind, called mind's essence, has two aspects, parts, or factors as they are called. One is emptiness and the other is knowing. Luminosity is a metaphor for the fundamental knowing quality of the essence of mind. It is sometimes translated as "clear light" but that is a mistake that comes from not understanding how the words of the Sanskrit and the Tibetan, too, go together. It does not refer to a light that has the quality of clearness (something that makes no sense, actually!) but refers to the illuminative property which is the hallmark of mind. Mind knows, that is what it does. Metaphorically, it is a luminosity that illuminates its own content. In both Sanskrit and Tibetan Buddhist literature, the term is frequently abbreviated just to gsal ba, "clarity", with the same meaning.

Mind, Skt. chitta, Tib. sems: the complicated process of mind which occurs because there is ignorance. This sort of mind is a samsaric phenomenon. It is a dualistic mind.

Mindfulness, Tib. dran pa: A particular mental event, one that has the ability to keep mind on its object. Together with alertness, it is one of the two causes of developing shamatha. See alertness for a explanation.

Post-attainment, Tib. rjes thob: see "Equipoise and post-attainment".

Preserve, Tib. skyong ba: An important term in both Mahāmudrā and Great Completion. In general, it means to defend, protect, nurture, maintain. In the higher tantras it means to keep something just as it is, to nurture that something so that it stays and is not lost. Also, in the higher tantras, it is often used in reference to preserving the state where the state is some particular state of being. Because of this, the phrase "preserve the state" is an important instruction in the higher tantras.

Rigpa, Tib. rig pa: This is the singularly most important term in the whole of Great Completion and Mahāmudrā. In particular, it is the key word of all words in the Great Completion system of the Thorough Cut. Rigpa literally means to know in the sense of "I see!" It is used at all levels of meaning from the coarsest everyday sense of knowing something to the deepest sense of knowing something as presented in the system of Thorough Cut. The system of Thorough Cut uses this term in a very special sense, though it still retains its basic meaning of "to know". To translate it as "awareness" which is common practice these days is a poor practice; there are many kinds of awareness but there is only one rigpa and besides, rigpa is substantially more than just awareness. Since this is such an important term and since it lacks an equivalent in English, I choose not to translate it. However, it will be helpful in reading the text to understanding the meaning as just given.

This is the term used to indicate enlightened mind as experienced by the practitioner on the path of these practices. The term itself specifically refers to the dynamic knowing quality of mind. It absolutely does not mean a simple registering, as implied by the word "awareness" which unfortunately is often used to translate this term. There is no word in English that exactly matches it, though the idea of "seeing" or "insight on the spot" is very close. Proof of this is found in the fact that the original Sanskrit term "vidyā" is actually the root of all words in English that start with "vid" and mean "to see", for example, "video", "vision", and so on. Chogyam Trungpa Rinpoche, who was particular skilled at getting Tibetan words into English, also stated that this term rigpa really did not have a good equivalent in English, though he thought that "insight" was the closest. My own conclusion after hearing extensive teaching on it is that rigpa is just best left untranslated. However, it will be helpful in reading the text to understanding the meaning as just given. Note that rigpa has both noun and verb forms. To get the verb form, I use "rigpa'ing".

State, Tib. ngang: A key term in Mahāmudrā and Great Completion. Unfortunately it is often not translated and in so doing much meaning is lost. Alternatively, it is often translated as "within" which is incorrect. The term means a "state". A state is a certain, ongoing situation. In Buddhist meditation in general, there are various states that a practitioner has to enter and remain in as part of developing the meditation.

Thorough Cut, Tib. khregs chod: the Dzogchen system has several levels to it. The innermost level has two main practices, the first called Thregcho which literally translates as Thorough Cut and the second called Thogal which translates as Direct Crossing. The meaning of Thorough Cut has been misunderstood. The meaning is clearly explained in the *Illuminator Tibetan-English Dictionary*:

> "Thorough Cut is a practice in which the solidification that sentient beings produce by having rational minds which grasp at a perceived object and perceiving subject is sliced through so as to get the underlying reality which has always been present in the essence of mind and which is called Alpha Purity in this system of teachings. For this reason, Thorough Cut is also known as Alpha Purity Thorough Cut."

The etymology of the word is explained in the Great Completion teachings either as ཁྲེགས་སུ་ཆོད་པ་ or ཁྲེགས་གི་ཆོད་པ་. In either case, the term ཆོད་པ་ is "a cut"; there are all sorts of different "cuts" and this is one of them. Then, in the case of ཁྲེགས་སུ་ཆོད་པ་, ཁྲེགས་སུ་ is an adverb modifying the verb "to cut" and has the meaning of making the cut fully, completely. It is explained with the example of slicing off a finger. A finger could be sliced with a sharp knife such that the cut was not quite complete and the cut off portion was left hanging. Alternatively, it could be sliced through in one, decisive movement such that the finger was completely and definitely severed. That kind of thorough cut is what is meant here. In the case of ཁྲེགས་གྲོ་ཆོད་པ, the term ཁྲེགས་གྲོ is as an adverb that has the meaning of something that is doubtless, of something that is unquestionably so. A translation based on the first explanation would be "Thorough Cut" and on the second would be "Decisive Cut".

Other translations that have been put forward for this term are: "Cutting Resistance" and "Cutting Solidity". Of these, "Cutting Resistance" is usually a translation made on the basis of students expressing the "resistance to practice", etcetera. That is a complete misunderstanding of the term. The term means that that the practitioner of this system cuts *decisively* through rational mind, regardless of its degree of solidity, so as to arrive directly at the essence of mind.

Unaltered or uncontrived, Tib. ma bcos pa: The opposite of "altered" and "contrived". Something which has not been altered from its native state; something which has been left just as it is.

Vipashyana, Tib. lhag mthong: The Sanskrit name for one of the two main practices of meditation needed in the Buddhist system for gaining insight into reality. The other one, shamatha, keeps the mind focussed while this one, vipaśhyanā, looks piercingly into the nature of things.

Wisdom, Skt. jñāna, Tib. ye shes: This is a fruition term that refers to the kind of mind, the kind of knower possessed by a buddha. The original Sanskrit term has many meanings but overall has the sense of just knowing. In Buddhism, it refers to the most basic type of knowing possible. Sentient beings could do this but their minds are obscured so, although they have the potential for knowing with the wisdom of a buddha, it does not happen. If they practise the path to buddhahood, at some point they will leave behind their obscuration and start knowing in this very simple and immediate way.

This sort of knowing is there at the core of every being's mind. Therefore, the Tibetans called it "the particular type of awareness which is always there". Because of their wording, it is often called "primordial wisdom" but that is too much. It simply means wisdom in the sense of the most fundamental knowing possible.

TIBETAN TEXT

༄༅། །རིག་དོ་སྐྱོང་ཐབས་ཨེ་ཤེས་སྙིང་པོ་བཞུགས་སོ།།

༄༅། །དཔལ་གདོད་མའི་མགོན་པོ་ལ་ཕྱག་འཚལ་ལོ། །རིག་དོ་སྐྱོང་
བ་ལ། དོ་ཤེས་རྒྱལ་རྟོགས་བཏུན་པ་ཐོབ་པ་གསུམ་རིམ་གྱིས་འོང་བས།
དང་པོ་བླ་མའི་མན་ངག་གིས་རིག་པའི་རང་ཞལ་རྟེན་པ་ཡིན་དུ་སྤྱོད་དང་ཐུབ་ཏེ།
མཐོང་བའི་བར་དུ་ཞུན་ཐར་བཅད། ཐག་ཆོད་ནས་རང་གིས་དེ་ཡི་ཌི་ དོ་པོ་
སྐྱོང་བ་ཁོན་གསལ་ཆེ་སྟེ། དོ་ཤེས་པ་ཚམ་གྱིས་མི་ཚོག་སྟེ་རྒྱལ་རྟོགས་དགོས།
དེ་ཡང་དང་པོར་རིག་དོ་ཤེས་ཀྱང་དེ་ཐོག་མ་བཞག་ན་རྣམ་རྟོག་གིས་བར་བཅད་
ནས་རིག་པ་རྟེན་པར་འཆར་དགར་འོང་སྟེ། དེ་དུས་རྣམ་རྟོག་ལ་དགག་སྒྲུབ་
མེད་པར་བཞག་ནས་རིག་པ་མ་བཅོས་པའི་དང་དུ་ཡང་ཡང་འཇོག་ཡུན་བསྲིང་བ
གལ་ཆེ། དེ་ལྟར་ཡང་ཡང་གོམས་ནས་རྣམ་རྟོག་གི་ཟ་ཀྲབས་ཤུགས་ཇེ་ཆུང་
དང་རིག་དོ་ཇེ་གསལ་སྐྱོང་བདེ་བྱུང་ན། མཐམ་གཞག་ཏུ་དེའི་ཐོག་ཏུ་ཅི་
གནས་དང་། རྗེས་ཐོབ་རིག་དོ་དྲན་པའི་དྲན་པ་བཟེན། དེ་ལ་གོམས་ན་
རིག་པའི་རྒྱལ་ཇེ་རྟོགས་སུ་འགྲོ་སྟེ། དང་པོར་རྣམ་རྟོག་ཤར་ཀྱང་དེ་འགོག

13

བྱེད་གཉེན་པོ་གཞན་བརྟེན་མི་དགོས་པར། རང་མལ་དུ་བཞག་པས་ཡུད་ཙམ་
ན་རང་གྲོལ་བ་སྒྱུལ་གྱི་མདུད་པ་རང་གིས་རང་བཤིག་པ་ལྟ་བུ་འབྱུང་། སྨྲ་
ཡང་གོམས་པས་རྣམ་ 〔 ༣ 〕 རྟོག་ཤར་བས་ཅུང་ཟད་རེ་རྟོགས་ཀྱང་དེ་མ་ཐག་
རང་ཡལ་དུ་འགྲོ་བ་རྒྱ་ལ་རི་མོ་བྲིས་པ་ལྟ་བུ་འབྱུང་། དེ་དང་གོམས་པས་
རྣམ་རྟོག་ཤར་བས་ཅི་ཡང་མི་གནོད་པས་ཤར་མ་ཤར་གྱི་རེ་དོགས་མེད་པ་ཁང་
སྟོང་དུ་རྐུན་མ་ཞུགས་པ་ལྟ་བུ་ཕན་གནོད་མེད་པའི་ཉམས་འཆར། དེ་དང་
གོམས་པས་རྩལ་རྫོགས་པ་མཐར་ཕྱིན་སྟེ་མཐར་རྣམ་རྟོག་དང་ཀུན་གཞི་འགྱུ་
བྱེད་ཀྱི་རླུང་དང་བཅས་པ་མ་བཅོས་ཆོས་སྐུར་ཐིམ་ནས་རིག་པ་རང་སར་ཟིན།
གསེར་སྐྱིང་ན་ས་རྡོ་ཐལ་བ་བཅལ་ཀྱང་མི་རྙེད་པ་ལྟར་སྱང་སྱིད་མ་ལུས་པ་ཆོས་
སྐུའི་ཞིང་དུ་ཤར་ཏེ་དག་པ་རབ་འབྱམས་སུ་སོང་བའི་ཚེ་ན་བརྟན་པ་ཐོབ་པ་ཞེས་
བྱ་སྟེ། འཁོར་འདས་དང་སྐྱེ་འཆིའི་རེ་དོགས་རྩད་ནས་ཞིག་པའོ། །དེ་
ལྟར་ཉིན་སྲང་རྣམ་རྟོག་རིག་པའི་དབང་དུ་འདུས་པའི་གོ་རིམ་བཞིན་མཚན་མོར་
ཡང་གདམས་ངག་གཞན་བརྟེན་མི་དགོས་པར། རྨི་ལམ་དང་སྒྲབ་འཐུག་གི་
འོད་གསལ་ཟིན་པ་སོགས་ཆ་མཚུངས་འོང་བ་ཞེས་པར་བྱས་ལ་ཅི་ནས་བརྟན་པ་
མ་ཐོབ་བར་དུ་ཡེངས་མེད་ཀྱི་བཙོན་པ་རྒྱ་པོའི་རྒྱུན་ལྟར་ 〔 ༣ 〕 མཐུད་དགོས་
སོ། །མི་ཐམ་པས་གདམས་པ་དགེ་ལེགས་འཕེལ། དགེའོ།། ॥